Hello!

Written by Lisa Thompson

Pictures by Luke Jurevicius and Arthur Moody

I can see Nuggle.

Hello, Nuggle.

I can see Gog.

Hello, Gog.

I can see Dash.

Hello, Dash.

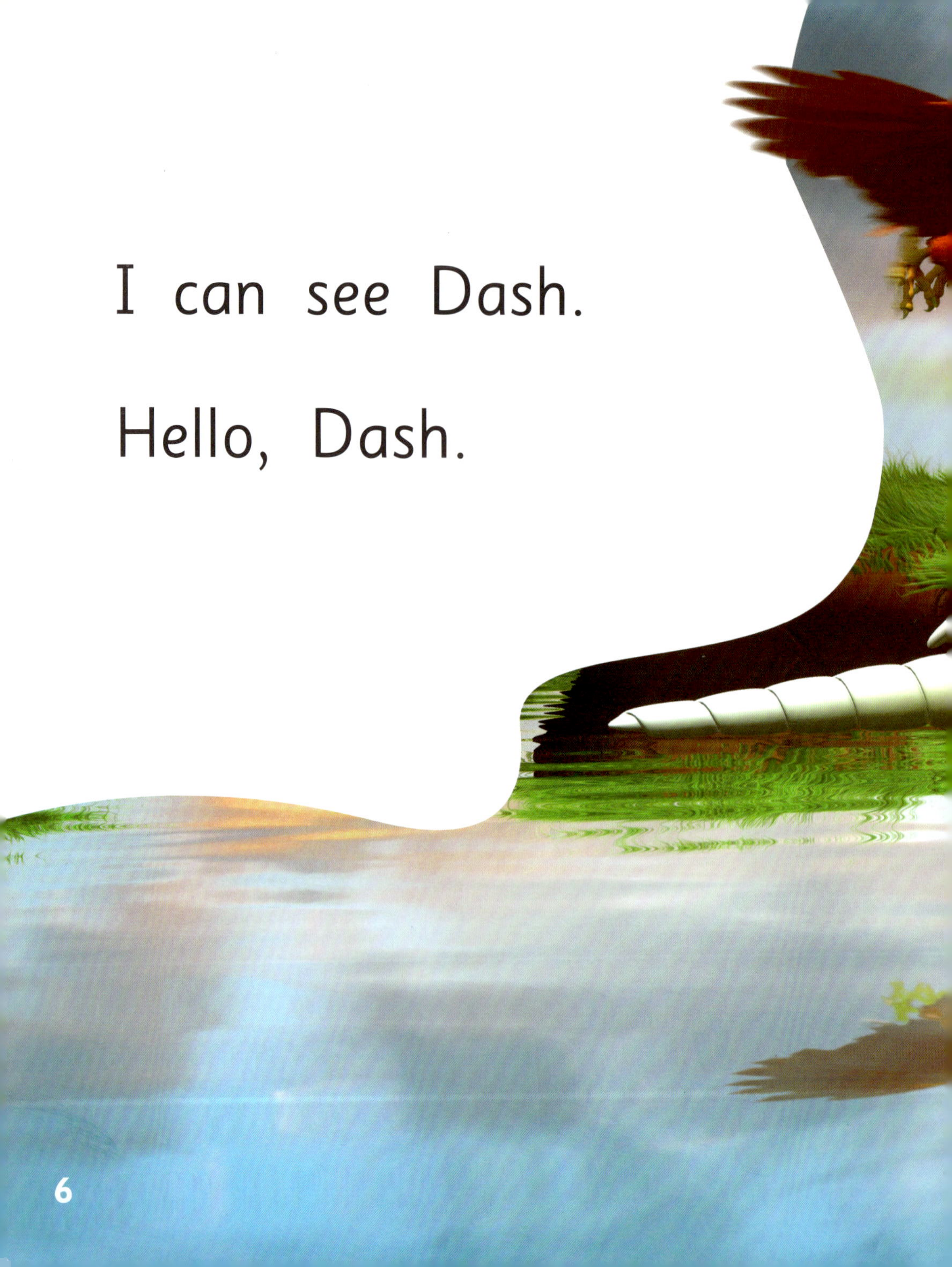

I can see Tufty.

Hello, Tufty.

I can see Hector.

Hello, Hector.

I can see Binks.

Hello, Binks.

I can see Boo.

Hello, Boo.

Boo!

I can see Gog.

I can see Binks.

I can see Nuggle.